"In an ever-changing world—what a comfort that God and His Word never change. I can honestly say that I have never regretted spending time in the Word. There has never been a time that the Scriptures didn't bring refreshment and hope. I encourage you to dive into the truth of the Scriptures that are found in these pages. God bless."

Michael W. Smith, Singer/Songwriter

"These books take you from the ordinary to the extraordinary."

Chris Sanders, Former Tennessee Titans Wide Receiver and 11-Time Track All-American

R̽

DOSAGE FOR A HAPPIER LIFE:

Day One: Read entire book 1 time through (Should take 15 minutes or less.)

Day Two and Beyond: Read OUT LOUD the Bible Passages ONLY, at least 2 times per day.

USA $8.99

About the Autho

June H. Olin is a Christian author and speaker who dedicates her life to extolling the medicinal aspects of the Holy Bible. June, her husband and four children live in Franklin, Tn.

S0-AFB-274

Rx

Prescription for
HAPPINESS

June H. Olin

Published by June H. Olin

PMB 120

2020 Fieldstone Parkway, Suite 900

Franklin, TN 37069

Printed in the United States of America

Library of Congress Control Number 2005902323

ISBN 0-976447-0-8

Scripture quotations are taken from and used by permission, all rights reserved: *The Amplified Bible* (AMP). *The Amplified Bible, Old Testament.* Copyright © 1965, 1987 by Zondervan Corporation. *The Amplified Bible, New Testament,* Copyright 1958, 1987 by the Lockman Foundation. ** *The Holy Bible, New International Version* (NIV). Copyright © 1973, 1978, 1984 by International Bible Society. Used by permission of Zondervan Publishing House. ** *The New King James Version* (NKJV). Copyright © 1982 by Thomas Nelson, Inc. ** *The Holy Bible, New Living Translation* (NLT) Copyright © 1996 Tyndale House Publishers, Inc. Wheaton, Illinois 60189.

Author's Note – In certain translations, some publishers have not capitalized pronouns referring to God and Jesus. We apologize for the confusion.

ACKNOWLEDGMENTS

First, I'd like to thank the Author of this book, Jesus Christ. Without Him, I am nothing.

I'd like to extend my heartfelt appreciation to my "Mama" who never stopped encouraging me to write the Rx books.

A big thank you to Anne Severance, my editor and friend. May God bless you for your gift of time and expertise in editing this book. Many thanks to Susan Dobbins for her artistic and creative input.

Without the many prayers and fastings from my Mom, Barbara Holley, and my sisters, Chanda Will, Jodie Snell and Zodie Horton, these books would not be in existence.

My children, Ryan, David, Jacobie and Sinclair, thank you for your patience with me writing 'round the clock. Also, I'd like to thank each of you for your creative ideas, all of which were used in creating these books. I love you guys!

And last, I'd like to honor my soul mate and very best friend in the whole world, my husband Jim. Your prayers, weekly fasting, and your confidence in me gave me the fuel to press forward and fulfill my calling to write this book. Thank you from the bottom of my heart.

INTRODUCTION

Grab yourself a cup of coffee or a hot tea. Now follow me to my back porch and let's get acquainted in my well worn, yet favorite green rocking chairs. I want to share with you my secret for overcoming unhappiness and sadness. It works, and with no side effects!

Once upon a time . . . I had been grappling with a lifelong problem of insecurity. I made many fruitless attempts at trying to overcome this debilitating "illness". Finally, through the inspiration of the Holy Spirit, I figured out the prescription that would cure my insecurities, once and for all! I collected every verse in the Bible that pertained to "my" problem and compiled them into a little book. This book became my best friend and I read it over and over, saturating my mind with God's Word. Whether standing in the grocery checkout, waiting in the car-pool line, or sitting on an airplane, I was reading and absorbing these very powerful, potent words that would eventually make me whole again!

A transformation began to occur... **I WAS CURED!!**

When others started to notice the "new me," I proceeded to tell them about my little book and its healing power. I even volunteered to write one for their special need. Many took me up on the offer. I would no more be finished with one book before another one was requested. I witnessed miracles through the use of these "little books"; therefore, I knew I had to get them out to the "world" so that people could begin living the same life of freedom in Christ that I had discovered.

Through much prayer and fasting, the Holy Spirit led me to this first book, Rx for Happiness. I worked constantly, searching for the most important Scriptures on happiness. Once the passages were all collected, I felt led to give a brief interpretation on how that Scripture could be applied to one's life!

Before I wrote my first words, something very disappointing occurred. My awesome hubby and I started to argue over everything that could be argued about. If he said, "The sky is blue," I would say, "No, it's black," and vice versa. We argued over "nit noid" things of absolutely no importance! During this excruciating period with my husband, I still attempted to write my Rx for Happiness book, but, of course, to no avail!

I awakened one Saturday morning, still agitated with my precious husband over who knows what, and informed him that there would be no book written. I proceeded to explain that I was miserable due to our marital tiffs and that I didn't believe God would call such a miserable woman to write a book on … Happiness! I almost cried at the thought of giving up this "thing" God had called me to do, so I asked my dear hubby if I could get the book out and follow the prescription for Happiness exactly as prescribed.

He agreed to sit with me and listen to the Scriptures. After I had read about half, I put the Scriptures on my lap, turned to him and asked sarcastically, "Do you feel any 'happier?'" "Yes, as a matter of fact, I do!" he replied. "How 'bout you?" I paused, lowered my pride, and admitted, "Yes. I do!"

I realized, at that moment, if I were to write a general prescription for the world, it would have to work on me . . . every time! I began reading the "Happiness" Scriptures twice a day and, instantly, my husband and I stopped arguing, even in the midst of a very stressful time in our lives.

I am here to tell you God's Word works! It is alive and powerful and is the only foolproof prescription for living . . . *happily ever after.*

Now, believe me, my new friend, my past life has been nowhere near a fairy tale. That's why, out of desperation, I turned to God's pure Word to get help. I learned that I had to say the Scriptures **out loud** two to three times a day to get real results.

Please listen to me. I have written these books just for you so that you don't have to make as many mistakes, and live in such bondage as I once did! If you will follow the prescription I have written, exactly as directed, I am confident that your victory is just around the corner!

It's time to dive into this little book, carry it with you wherever you go and be sure to take all the prescribed Scriptures at least twice a day.

Please e-mail me at <u>Info@Rxbooks.com</u> with your good news. I look forward to hearing from you! God bless you, my brother or sister in Christ.

PRAYER NOTES
for a
NEW BEGINNING

Today, God's Word spoke this to me_____

_____

_____

_____

_____

_____

I will let go of_____

_____

_____

_____

_____

I will begin by_____

_____

_____

_____

¹²**For the word of God is living and powerful, and sharper than any two-edged sword, piercing even to the division of soul and spirit, and of joints and marrow, and is a discerner of the thoughts and intents of the heart.**

Hebrews 4:12 (NKJV)

This Scripture is the basis for the "Rx" books because when you are sick (emotionally, spiritually, or physically), you need a prescription for something that will improve your health. God's Word is more alive and powerful than any drug, doctor or therapist. It is life, and contains all answers to life's questions.

If you will use Scripture as a mandatory tool for your life, your journey on Earth will prosper in peace, happiness and completeness… regardless of your circumstances.

Please, I beg of you, read and reread these passages. Get ready, my dear, for a perpetual smile upon your face.

PRAYER NOTES
for a
NEW BEGINNING

Today, God's Word spoke this to me _____

_____

_____

_____

_____

_____

I will let go of _____

_____

_____

_____

_____

I will begin by _____

_____

_____

_____

¹³Shout for joy, O heavens; rejoice,
O earth; burst into song, O mountains!
For the LORD comforts his people and will
have compassion on his afflicted ones.

Isaiah 49:13 (NIV)

*I can hardly contain myself when I read this Scripture. I shout **out
loud** these living words and I cry tears of joy for the sheer excitement I
have in Him!*

*My precious friend, the Lord will fill you to the brim with comfort, a
comfort that only He can offer. Ask Him for it…I dare you!*

PRAYER NOTES
for a
NEW BEGINNING

Today, God's Word spoke this to me_____

_____

_____

_____

_____

_____

I will let go of_____

_____

_____

_____

_____

I will begin by_____

_____

_____

_____

¹¹**You will show me the path of life;**
in Your presence is fullness of joy;
at Your right hand are
pleasures forevermore.

Psalm 16:11 (NKJV)

Have you ever felt like you had no idea which direction you should be taking in your life? Well, here it is, the answer you've been waiting for. Follow closely behind the Lord. Stay near (in prayer and in His Word), or you'll get lost. He takes lots of twists and turns, but, believe me, my dear, the trip is never boring and He's always right on the mark. Enjoy your journey.

PRAYER NOTES
for a
NEW BEGINNING

Today, God's Word spoke this to me_____

_____

_____

_____

_____

_____

I will let go of_____

_____

_____

_____

_____

I will begin by_____

_____

_____

_____

¹³**May the God of your hope so fill you with all joy and peace in believing [through the experience of your faith] that by the power of the Holy Spirit you may abound and be overflowing (bubbling over) with hope.**

Romans 15:13 (AMP)

I sure wouldn't mind having so much hope and joy that I just couldn't stand it. Can you imagine saying, "Hey, Lord, take back some of these blessings; I'm overwhelmed at the moment!" Well, sister or brother, get ready . . . the Holy Spirit is loaded with peace and joy and is ready to fire in your direction. Ask to see some of His mighty power!

PRAYER NOTES
for a
NEW BEGINNING

Today, God's Word spoke this to me_____

_____

_____

_____

_____

I will let go of_____

_____

_____

_____

_____

I will begin by_____

_____

_____

_____

³⁰**And you shall love the L**ORD
your God with all your heart,
with all your soul, with all your mind,
and with all your strength.
This is the first commandment.

Mark 12:30 (NKJV)

I cannot stress enough, my friend, to ask, beg and plead for the Lord to
rain down on you a supernatural, unconditional love for Him. Tell
Him you want to experience a love affair with Him, like none other!
Get ready to fall blissfully in love with Jesus.

PRAYER NOTES
for a
NEW BEGINNING

Today, God's Word spoke this to me_____

_____

_____

_____

_____

_____

I will let go of_____

_____

_____

_____

_____

I will begin by_____

_____

_____

_____

⁸I know the LORD is always with me.
I will not be shaken,
for he is right beside me.
⁹No wonder my heart is filled with joy, and
my mouth shouts his praises!
My body rests in safety.

Psalm 16:8-9 (NLT)

Guess what? You can NOT be shaken or moved if you have given your life to Jesus. Yes, you'll have trouble in this life, but because He is always at your side, rest in the knowledge that He'll never leave you. Whatever difficulties you have to endure, take comfort in this, that He'll carry you through them. Give Him a "high five" at this moment!

PRAYER NOTES
for a
NEW BEGINNING

Today, God's Word spoke this to me_____

_____

_____

_____

_____

I will let go of_____

_____

_____

_____

_____

I will begin by_____

_____

_____

_____

²⁴This is the day which the LORD has made; we will rejoice and be glad in it.

Psalm 118:24 (NKJV)

I can remember many days in my life when I have not experienced much joy or happiness. I have felt unloved at various times in my life, but thanks to the Word of God and my tenacity in saturating my mind with His Word, I now KNOW I am loved by Him and many others!

Let's celebrate our lives and the fact that you and I are so cherished and unconditionally loved by Jesus Christ. My dear, take pleasure and satisfaction in Him today!

PRAYER NOTES
for a
NEW BEGINNING

Today, God's Word spoke this to me_____

_____

_____

_____

_____

_____

I will let go of _____

_____

_____

_____

_____

I will begin by_____

_____

_____

_____

3"To console those who mourn in Zion,
to give them beauty for ashes,
the oil of joy for mourning,
the garment of praise for the spirit of
heaviness; that they may be called trees of
righteousness, the planting of the LORD,
that He may be glorified."

Isaiah 61:3 (NKJV)

Whatever the "bad" is in your life, God will work it together for His "good," no matter how difficult, scary or horrible the situation might be! The King of kings can and will make it right. Give it to God. Lay it before His throne and leave it there!

PRAYER NOTES
for a
NEW BEGINNING

Today, God's Word spoke this to me_____

_____

_____

_____

_____

_____

I will let go of_____

_____

_____

_____

_____

_____

I will begin by_____

_____

_____

_____

²⁵"And the rain descended,
the floods came, and the winds blew
and beat on that house;
and it did not fall,
for it was founded on the rock."

Matthew 7:25 (NKJV)

Your own personal "rains," "floods" and "tornadoes" will come as part of life, but, praise God, my friend, you will NOT fall because Jesus Christ is your foundation!

PRAYER NOTES
for a
NEW BEGINNING

Today, God's Word spoke this to me_____

_____

_____

_____

_____

I will let go of_____

_____

_____

_____

_____

I will begin by_____

_____

_____

_____

¹³Happy (blessed, fortunate, enviable) is the man who finds skillful and godly Wisdom, and the man who gets understanding [drawing it forth from God's Word and life's experiences],
¹⁴for the gaining of it is better than the gaining of silver, and the profit of it better than fine gold.

Proverbs 3:13-14 (AMP)

Owners' manuals are provided for almost everything we own (i.e. our new cars, appliances, lawnmowers, etc.). The Bible is the owner's manual for our lives. Period! It tells us what to eat, how to have thriving marriages, how to manage our money, and how to be happy and healthy! Dust off your Manual, follow the instructions carefully and bask in the warmth of God's love. Given your newfound wisdom and your total confidence in His Son Jesus, attack this world with your eyes wide open!

PRAYER NOTES
for a
NEW BEGINNING

Today, God's Word spoke this to me_____

_____

_____

_____

_____

_____

I will let go of_____

_____

_____

_____

_____

_____

I will begin by_____

_____

_____

_____

_____

¹⁷Her [wisdom's] ways
are ways of pleasantness,
and all her paths are peace.
¹⁸She is a tree of life to those
who take hold of her, and happy are all
who retain her.

Proverbs 3:17-18 (NKJV)

Godly wisdom brings forth peace, happiness and a fulfilled life. Do you know how to gain that wisdom? My precious friend, go find a Bible (one that's easy to read) and begin your journey in the Book of John. Keep reading every single day of your life! God's wisdom will be imparted to you, my dear. It won't be long before you'll witness modern-day miracles in your life!

PRAYER NOTES
for a
NEW BEGINNING

Today, God's Word spoke this to me_____

_____

_____

_____

_____

I will let go of_____

_____

_____

_____

_____

I will begin by_____

_____

_____

_____

²**Consider it pure joy, my brothers, whenever you face trials of many kinds, ³because you know that the testing of your faith develops perseverance. ⁴Perseverance must finish its work so that you may be mature and complete, not lacking anything.**

James 1:2-4 (NIV)

There is nothing sweeter than succeeding in something you used to "stink" at! Right? The old saying, "No Pain, No Gain," really is true when it comes to our relationship with Jesus. God knows the only way we can grow up and mature in Him is through our many "stinks" and mistakes that have been turned into successes. Friend, use the healing of your weaknesses as a platform to shout out your victory!

PRAYER NOTES
for a
NEW BEGINNING

Today, God's Word spoke this to me_____

_____

_____

_____

_____

_____

I will let go of _____

_____

_____

_____

_____

I will begin by_____

_____

_____

_____

_____

¹³I can do all things through Christ who strengthens me.

Philippians 4:13 (NKJV)

How many things can we do through Christ? None? A few? Some? Not many? A lot? No, my friend, you are capable of doing ALL things through the strength of the One and Only Jesus Christ!

PRAYER NOTES
for a
NEW BEGINNING

Today, God's Word spoke this to me _____

_____

_____

_____

_____

I will let go of _____

_____

_____

_____

_____

I will begin by _____

_____

_____

_____

_____

¹⁸When I said, My foot is slipping, Your mercy and loving-kindness,
O Lord, held me up.
¹⁹In the multitude of my [anxious] thoughts within me,
Your comforts cheer and delight my soul!

Psalm 94:18-19 (AMP)

Have you ever been so nervous and filled with such anxiety that you knew any moment you could just collapse? I've been there, and if you haven't, you probably will at some point in your life! During that most difficult period, my Lord held me so tenderly, like a newborn babe. It wasn't until I relinquished it all to Him that He could fully comfort me. I finally let go and let God take over! My friend, please realize there is no situation too complicated for the Lord. I speak from personal experience!

PRAYER NOTES
for a
NEW BEGINNING

Today, God's Word spoke this to me_____

_____

_____

_____

_____

_____

I will let go of_____

_____

_____

_____

_____

I will begin by_____

_____

_____

_____

²⁴Up to this time you have not
asked a [single] thing in My Name
[as presenting all that I AM];
but now ask and keep on asking and you
will receive, so that your joy (gladness,
delight) may be full and complete.

John 16:24 (AMP)

I love the "keep on asking" part of this Scripture, because our Lord is saying to be persistent! Don't give up! Don't EVER give up! Because you WILL receive that blessing and then your happiness will be complete.

PRAYER NOTES
for a
NEW BEGINNING

Today, God's Word spoke this to me_____

_____

_____

_____

_____

_____

I will let go of_____

_____

_____

_____

_____

_____

I will begin by_____

_____

_____

_____

_____

³¹But those who wait for the Lord [who expect, look for, and hope in Him] shall change and renew their strength and power; they shall lift their wings and mount up [close to God] as eagles [mount up to the sun]; they shall run and not be weary, they shall walk and not faint or become tired.

Isaiah 40:31 (AMP)

Our journey with the Lord is a marathon. Please, my dear, stop trying to make it into a "50-yard dash". I promise from the bottom of my heart and soul that God will give you the strength and endurance you will need to complete life's marathon with Him!

P.S. Get ready to receive the "gold medal," because He ALWAYS wins the race!

PRAYER NOTES
for a
NEW BEGINNING

Today, God's Word spoke this to me_____

_____

_____

_____

_____

_____

I will let go of_____

_____

_____

_____

_____

I will begin by_____

_____

_____

_____

_____

¹⁰**Even the strong young lions
sometimes go hungry,
but those who trust in the Lord will
never lack any good thing.**

Psalm 34:10 (NLT)

A strong, young lion, especially one that is hungry, is more powerful than any creature on Earth, but this ferocious lion pales in comparison to the omnipotence of our Savior. With God on your side, you will NEVER go hungry.

PRAYER NOTES
for a
NEW BEGINNING

Today, God's Word spoke this to me_____

_____

_____

_____

_____

I will let go of_____

_____

_____

_____

_____

I will begin by_____

_____

_____

_____

¹O GOD, You are my God, earnestly will I seek You; my inner self thirsts for You, my flesh longs and is faint for You, in a dry and weary land where no water is. ²So I have looked upon You in the sanctuary to see Your power and Your glory. ³Because Your loving-kindness is better than life, my lips shall praise You. ⁴So will I bless You while I live; I will lift up my hands in Your name. ⁵My whole being shall be satisfied as with marrow and fatness; and my mouth shall praise You with joyful lips.

Psalm 63:1-5 (AMP)

Man, if you aren't already longing and yearning for your Lord, then ask Him, right now, to give you such a thirst and hunger for Him. Ask Him to let your spiritual stomach growl out of craving for Him. He will give you that insatiable appetite. And in return, you will have an endless buffet of peace, joy and contentment!

PRAYER NOTES
for a
NEW BEGINNING

Today, God's Word spoke this to me_____

_____

_____

_____

_____

_____

I will let go of_____

_____

_____

_____

_____

I will begin by_____

_____

_____

_____

¹How happy are those who fear
the LORD — all who follow his ways!
²You will enjoy the fruit of your labor.
How happy you will be!
How rich your life!

Psalm 128:1-2 (NLT)

To fear God does not mean to shake and tremble in His presence.
On the contrary, my friend, a healthy fear is having the utmost respect
for Him, setting Him in His rightful place of authority, and maintaining
an ever- present knowledge of His omnipotence! With this knowledge,
fear Him, dear one. Follow Him and take hold of your free gift . . .
His happiness! Grab it. . . don't let go!

PRAYER NOTES
for a
NEW BEGINNING

Today, God's Word spoke this to me_____

_____

_____

_____

_____

I will let go of _____

_____

_____

_____

_____

I will begin by_____

_____

_____

_____

¹³**A happy heart makes the face cheerful,
but heartache crushes the spirit.**

Proverbs 15:13 (NIV)

*Laugh 'til your tummy hurts! Laugh out loud. Think of someone
who makes you smile and smile real big, from the inside out!
God loves your precious laughter, dear one. It's joyous music to
His ears!*

PRAYER NOTES
for a
NEW BEGINNING

Today, God's Word spoke this to me_____

_____

_____

_____

_____

I will let go of_____

_____

_____

_____

_____

I will begin by_____

_____

_____

_____

¹How good and how pleasant it is when brothers live together in unity!

Psalm 133:1 (NIV)

From firsthand experience, I know, my dear, how difficult (at times impossible) it is to live at peace with one another. But it is imperative that we do! No ifs, ands, or buts about it, you are commanded to: "Love your neighbor as yourself." The only way, and I mean ONLY way, is to ask Jesus to love "them" through you, 'cause you "ain't" going to be able to do it yourself. I challenge you to pray and ask for His love for those in your life who are not so lovable. You'll be amazed at the results!

PRAYER NOTES
for a
NEW BEGINNING

Today, God's Word spoke this to me_____

_____

_____

_____

_____

I will let go of_____

_____

_____

_____

_____

I will begin by_____

_____

_____

_____

⁹Blessed (enjoying enviable happiness, spiritually prosperous with life-joy and satisfaction in God's favor and salvation, regardless of their outward conditions) are the makers and maintainers of peace, for they shall be called the sons of God!

Matthew 5:9 (AMP)

My friend, when you are a peace-giver, you will certainly be a peace-receiver. With God's peace are His blessings of happiness and joy, no matter our circumstances. Praise God . . . He is so good!

PRAYER NOTES
for a
NEW BEGINNING

Today, God's Word spoke this to me_____

_____

_____

_____

_____

I will let go of_____

_____

_____

_____

_____

I will begin by_____

_____

_____

_____

¹⁶Be happy [in your faith]
and rejoice and be glad-hearted
continually (always).

1 Thessalonians 5:16 (AMP)

"Don't worry. . . be happy!" Remember that song? I used to sing it, but never really applied it to my life and to what Jesus says about being happy and content. I was like the "world," happy when all was well, yet miserable when all. . . wasn't! Thank You, God, for having a better plan for our lives: a plan of happiness, success and unexplained contentment regardless of our circumstances.

PRAYER NOTES
for a
NEW BEGINNING

Today, God's Word spoke this to me_____

_____

_____

_____

_____

I will let go of_____

_____

_____

_____

_____

I will begin by_____

_____

_____

_____

³³"I have told you these things,
so that in me you may have peace.
In this world you will have trouble.
But take heart!
I have overcome the world."

John 16:33 (NIV)

It's REAL simple!
Our world and all it has to offer = trials and sorrows.
JESUS = PEACE.

PRAYER NOTES
for a
NEW BEGINNING

Today, God's Word spoke this to me_____

_____

_____

_____

_____

_____

I will let go of_____

_____

_____

_____

_____

I will begin by_____

_____

_____

_____

⁹This is how God showed his
love among us:
He sent his one and only Son into the
world that we might live through him.
¹⁰This is love: not that we loved God, but
that he loved us and sent his Son as an
atoning sacrifice for our sins.

1 John 4:9-10 (NIV)

*I love my children with all of my heart and I can't even fathom
sacrificing them for a single second to save all of humanity. . .
I just can't! God did though! He sent His only Son for you and me,
my friend. He let Jesus be brutally tortured, and He allowed Him to
take on every single sin in this world so that you and I could live
victoriously and be forgiven for EVERYTHING! Take a minute to
give Him sincere thanks and praise!*

PRAYER NOTES
for a
NEW BEGINNING

Today, God's Word spoke this to me_____

_____

_____

_____

_____

_____

I will let go of_____

_____

_____

_____

_____

I will begin by_____

_____

_____

_____

^{10}"Likewise, I say to you,
there is joy in the presence of the angels of
God over one sinner who repents."

Luke 15:10 (NKJV)

*Do you understand what sin is? The Ten Commandments state,
"Thou shalt not murder," and the Bible tells us that when we harbor
anger toward someone, that is equivalent to murder. Also, the Ten
Commandments state, "Thou shalt not lie." Now be completely honest
with yourself: Haven't you told a "white lie" before, maybe even many
times? My dear, a lie is a lie, no matter how you deem it. God says,
"Do not lie." So, my friend, the first thing you should realize is that
according to the Ten Commandments … you DO sin. But, thank
Jesus, all you have to do to be forgiven is to ask Him to forgive you.
Then, you must turn away from that behavior. God will forgive you
over and over and ….*

PRAYER NOTES
for a
NEW BEGINNING

Today, God's Word spoke this to me_____

_____

_____

_____

_____

I will let go of_____

_____

_____

_____

_____

I will begin by_____

_____

_____

_____

⁸**The commandments of the LORD are right, bringing joy to the heart. The commands of the LORD are clear, giving insight to life.**

Psalm 19:8 (NLT)

The Ten Commandments are a mirror for us to look into so that we can see the reflection of our true selves. The commandments reveal sin in our lives that we cannot see through our own eyes. Take a moment and find Exodus 20, plus Matthew 5:20-48. Meditate on these verses and pray, asking Jesus to show you your shortcomings. Now ask for forgiveness and start living a joyous life because of your freedom in the "truth". Remember, Jesus says, "The truth shall set you free!"

PRAYER NOTES
for a
NEW BEGINNING

Today, God's Word spoke this to me_____

_____

_____

_____

_____

I will let go of_____

_____

_____

_____

_____

I will begin by_____

_____

_____

_____

¹⁹**The humble will be filled with
fresh joy from the LORD.
Those who are poor will rejoice in the
Holy One of Israel.**

Isaiah 29:19 (NLT)

*Please don't get down about your financial problems. Remember, my
dear, you are an heir to the richest Man in the world. But always stay
humble, for in doing so, you'll be greatest in the Kingdom of heaven.
Scream and shout for joy…dance and dance some more, because your
security is in Him.*

PRAYER NOTES
for a
NEW BEGINNING

Today, God's Word spoke this to me_____

_____

_____

_____

_____

I will let go of_____

_____

_____

_____

_____

I will begin by_____

_____

_____

_____

⁶But godliness with contentment
is great gain.
⁷For we brought nothing into the world,
and we can take nothing out of it.

1 Timothy 6:6-7 (NIV)

*Have you ever heard anyone on their deathbed say, "Boy, I wish
I had spent more time at the office?" Of course not! Your money,
your "toys" and your power will not get you to heaven. They won't
save your life; they won't even make you happy in the long run.
Only God will! Plain and simple: Make Him Lord of your life and
you will have it all!*

PRAYER NOTES
for a
NEW BEGINNING

Today, God's Word spoke this to me_____

_____

_____

_____

_____

I will let go of_____

_____

_____

_____

_____

I will begin by_____

_____

_____

_____

¹⁰If you keep My commandments [if you continue to obey My instructions], you will abide in My love and live on in it, just as I have obeyed My Father's commandments and live on in His love. ¹¹I have told you these things, that My joy and delight may be in you, and that your joy and gladness may be of full measure and complete and overflowing.

John 15:10-11 (AMP)

Did you know that the Ten Commandments, according to Jesus, can be summed up in just two? "'You shall love the Lord your God with all your heart, with all your soul, and with all your mind.' And the second one is, "'You shall love your neighbor as yourself.'" Begin "loving" God's way today, for in return He promises you an abundance of happiness and joy!

PRAYER NOTES
for a
NEW BEGINNING

Today, God's Word spoke this to me_____

_____

_____

_____

_____

_____

I will let go of_____

_____

_____

_____

_____

_____

I will begin by_____

_____

_____

_____

_____

⁷The LORD is my strength
and my shield; my heart trusts in him,
and I am helped. My heart leaps for joy
and I will give thanks to him in song.

Psalm 28:7 (NIV)

God wants the very best for you! He has treasures upon treasures on which your name is inscribed. All you have to do to lay claim to His treasures is give Him total custody of your life.

PRAYER NOTES
for a
NEW BEGINNING

Today, God's Word spoke this to me_____

_____

_____

_____

_____

I will let go of_____

_____

_____

_____

_____

I will begin by_____

_____

_____

_____

¹²They will be like a well-watered garden,
   and they will sorrow no more.
¹³Then maidens will dance and be glad,
   young men and old as well.
I will turn their mourning into gladness;
   I will give them comfort
   and joy instead of sorrow.

Jeremiah 31:12-13 (NIV)

My dear one, you may be struggling with a nasty divorce, or loneliness, or the loss of a job, or even the loss of a precious loved one...whatever your pain is, please give it to the Lord. He is the ONLY way that you will get through this dry and desolate time! He will embrace you through this season and rain down heavily His comfort, His happiness and His love.

PRAYER NOTES
for a
NEW BEGINNING

Today, God's Word spoke this to me_____

_____

_____

_____

_____

I will let go of_____

_____

_____

_____

_____

I will begin by_____

_____

_____

_____

²⁸**And we know that all things work together for good to those who love God, to those who are called according to His purpose.**

Romans 8:28 (NKJV)

Not some things, my dear, but ALL things end up working for the best in the lives of true lovers of Jesus Christ. I want all of my "mess-ups" to work out for the good in my life, don't you? Pursue a love affair with Jesus!

PRAYER NOTES
for a
NEW BEGINNING

Today, God's Word spoke this to me_____

_____

_____

_____

_____

I will let go of_____

_____

_____

_____

_____

I will begin by_____

_____

_____

_____

²⁰He who deals wisely and heeds [God's] word and counsel shall find good, and whoever leans on, trusts in, and is confident in the Lord — happy, blessed, and fortunate is he.

Proverbs 16:20 (AMP)

The Lord led my husband to move his company to Florida with his whole family in tow. We decided to remodel our future home, which was in dire need of updating. Unfortunately, we made this decision without seeking God's guidance first. Together with architects, kitchen designers, and a builder, we developed a plan of action. After the planning process, God showed me a Scripture in Deuteronomy 28:12 which instructs us not to borrow money. I prayed, "Lord, if You are speaking to me, then please let my husband know, too!" God sure did! We were both in agreement to halt what we had worked on so hard. And shortly thereafter we found out God's reason. Within two months of our first move, God led us to move AGAIN to yet another state.

Whew! Were we glad we hadn't made that massive renovation! We said "Yes" to His plan, even when it didn't make sense. God so deserves our obedience to Him. Ask Him first before you make ANY decision. It's easier to do it right the first time!

PRAYER NOTES
for a
NEW BEGINNING

Today, God's Word spoke this to me_____

_____

_____

_____

_____

_____

I will let go of_____

_____

_____

_____

_____

I will begin by_____

_____

_____

_____

⁸O taste and see that the Lord [our God] is good! Blessed (happy, fortunate, to be envied) is the man who trusts and takes refuge in Him.

Psalm 34:8 (AMP)

Wouldn't it be awesome to go to a restaurant where your favorite chef had prepared all your favorite meals? You would certainly taste some incredible mouth-watering delicacies. This is how it is to get a "taste" of Jesus. You'll desire more and more of Him just by merely sampling His affections. The difference between the "chef" and "Jesus" is… the chef will eventually tire of cooking for you, but Jesus, my dear, will provide everything you need for the rest of your life and throughout eternity!

PRAYER NOTES
for a
NEW BEGINNING

Today, God's Word spoke this to me_____

_____

_____

_____

_____

I will let go of_____

_____

_____

_____

_____

I will begin by_____

_____

_____

_____

_____

¹¹But let all who take refuge in
you be glad; let them ever sing for joy.
Spread your protection over them,
that those who love your name
may rejoice in you.

Psalm 5:11 (NIV)

What is refuge to you? Being protected or guarded from impending
danger? Calling out for help when in despair? Isn't it a joy, and,
certainly, a relief to know that you have some place to escape? My
friend, rejoice today in your safe place of refuge with the Lord.

PRAYER NOTES
for a
NEW BEGINNING

Today, God's Word spoke this to me_____

_____

_____

_____

_____

I will let go of_____

_____

_____

_____

_____

I will begin by_____

_____

_____

_____

⁵Many, O Lord my God,
are the wonderful works which
You have done, and Your thoughts
toward us; no one can compare with You!
If I should declare and speak of them,
they are too many to be numbered.

Psalm 40:5 (AMP)

You are so cherished by the Lord that it's impossible to imagine how much He thinks about you! What have you done to deserve so much attention? Absolutely nothing (just like me)! It's called unconditional love, a never-ending love without a single string attached! Revel in it!

PRAYER NOTES
for a
NEW BEGINNING

Today, God's Word spoke this to me_____

_____

_____

_____

_____

_____

I will let go of_____

_____

_____

_____

_____

I will begin by_____

_____

_____

_____

¹⁹"And I have given you authority over all the power of the enemy, and you can walk among snakes and scorpions and crush them. Nothing will injure you. ²⁰But don't rejoice just because evil spirits obey you; rejoice because your names are registered as citizens of heaven."

Luke 10:19-20 (NLT)

Boy, do you have some mighty power through the Lord Jesus! But, what you should be most happy about is . . . that you will spend all eternity in a place beyond imagination called heaven.

PRAYER NOTES
for a
NEW BEGINNING

Today, God's Word spoke this to me_____

_____

_____

_____

_____

I will let go of_____

_____

_____

_____

_____

I will begin by_____

_____

_____

_____

⁴May he give you the desire of your heart
and make all your plans succeed.
⁵We will shout for joy when you are
victorious and will lift up our banners in
the name of our God.
May the LORD grant all your requests.

Psalm 20:4-5 (NIV)

The Lord will give you the desires of your heart when you give Him YOUR heart! He longs for our hearts, my dear, he longs for our hearts....

PRAYER NOTES
for a
NEW BEGINNING

Today, God's Word spoke this to me_____

_____

_____

_____

_____

I will let go of_____

_____

_____

_____

_____

I will begin by_____

_____

_____

_____

³Yes, the LORD has done
amazing things for us! What joy!
⁴Restore our fortunes,
LORD, as streams renew the desert.
⁵Those who plant in tears
will harvest with shouts of joy.

Psalm 126:3-5 (NLT)

Let your mouth be full of laughter, for God will do great and mighty things for you, my precious one. He will revive the life that has been stolen from you. Shout, my dear, in your victory! Amen!

PRAYER NOTES
for a
NEW BEGINNING

Today, God's Word spoke this to me_____

_____

_____

_____

_____

_____

I will let go of_____

_____

_____

_____

_____

_____

I will begin by_____

_____

_____

_____

_____

⁵Your love, O L ORD, reaches to the
heavens, your faithfulness to the skies.
⁶Your righteousness is like the
mighty mountains, your justice
like the great deep. O L ORD, you preserve
both man and beast.

Psalm 36:5-6 (NIV)

*I just sing out this Scripture in church with my whole heart and soul!
Why? Because He loves me all the way to the heavens and I am the
"apple of His eye." You are, too, my friend…and don't ever forget it!*

PRAYER NOTES
for a
NEW BEGINNING

Today, God's Word spoke this to me_____

_____

_____

_____

_____

_____

I will let go of_____

_____

_____

_____

_____

_____

I will begin by_____

_____

_____

_____

_____

²⁴But none of these things move me; nor do I count my life dear to myself, so that I may finish my race with joy, and the ministry which I received from the Lord Jesus, to testify to the gospel of the grace of God.

Acts 20:24 (NKJV)

Paul (a former highly respected Jewish leader) is demonstrating his complete trust and contentment in the Lord by saying, "None of these things (imprisonment, people trying to murder him, etc.) move me...," because he has committed his ENTIRE life to teaching others about Jesus. Wow! You and I, like Paul, have a work to complete, too! Let's finish it with perfect joy and as God's champions.

PRAYER NOTES
for a
NEW BEGINNING

Today, God's Word spoke this to me_____

_____

_____

_____

_____

_____

I will let go of_____

_____

_____

_____

_____

I will begin by_____

_____

_____

_____

_____

¹**And Hannah prayed and said:
"My heart rejoices in the LORD;
my horn (strength) is exalted in the
LORD. I smile at my enemies,
because I rejoice in Your salvation."**

1 Samuel 2:1 (NKJV)

*When your heart is so full of love for God, you will gather your
strength from Him. Even your enemies won't get "under your skin"
because of your complete joy in Him! That, my friend, is worth a
lifelong love affair with Jesus!*

PRAYER NOTES
for a
NEW BEGINNING

Today, God's Word spoke this to me_____

_____

_____

_____

_____

_____

I will let go of_____

_____

_____

_____

_____

I will begin by_____

_____

_____

_____

⁶In this you greatly rejoice, though now for a little while you may have had to suffer grief in all kinds of trials. ⁷These have come so that your faith - of greater worth than gold, which perishes even though refined by fire - may be proved genuine and may result in praise, glory and honor when Jesus Christ is revealed.

1 Peter 1:6-7 (NIV)

When my sons were little, they begged for candy, sodas, and just about anything that contained sugar! I wanted to give them everything they desired, just to see them happy, but never at the expense of their good health. Often, my answer to them was, "No, my dear son."

God is the same kind of parent. He desires to give us every earthly thing we beg of Him, but He will never do it at the expense of our maturity. Sweetie, take a seat beside Jesus Christ on the roller coaster of life's ups and downs, so that you will be prepared for the Kingdom of God, for which you have been called.

PRAYER NOTES
for a
NEW BEGINNING

Today, God's Word spoke this to me_____

_____

_____

_____

_____

I will let go of_____

_____

_____

_____

_____

I will begin by_____

_____

_____

_____

²Do not conform any longer to the
pattern of this world, but be transformed
by the renewing of your mind.
Then you will be able to test and approve
what God's will is - his good,
pleasing and perfect will.

Romans 12:2 (NIV)

*The definition of transformed is: "To change structure, appearance or
character." We may want to change, but we have no idea how. The
answer is in the above Scripture: "By the renewing of your mind…"
Saturate your mind with the Bible. Pray. Listen to clean, uplifting
music. Watch wholesome TV and "hang" with godly people. Then,
you are guaranteed to become a new, more beautiful person!*

PRAYER NOTES
for a
NEW BEGINNING

Today, God's Word spoke this to me_____

_____

_____

_____

_____

_____

I will let go of_____

_____

_____

_____

_____

_____

I will begin by_____

_____

_____

_____

_____

¹Oh, the joys of those who do not
follow the advice of the wicked,
or stand around with sinners,
or join in with scoffers.
²But they delight in doing everything
the LORD wants;
day and night they think about his law.

Psalm 1:1-2 (NLT)

You know the old saying: "Birds of a feather flock together." When you
spend time with other believers, you grow in Jesus. Otherwise, you
open yourself up to serious problems. Stay far, far away from bad
influences. Pray for and love them, my friend, but keep your distance.
Remember, your Best Friend is Jesus . . . go have a blast with Him
today!

PRAYER NOTES
for a
NEW BEGINNING

Today, God's Word spoke this to me_____

_____

_____

_____

_____

_____

I will let go of_____

_____

_____

_____

_____

_____

I will begin by_____

_____

_____

_____

_____

**¹¹You will show me the way of life,
granting me the joy of your presence and
the pleasures of living with you forever.**

Psalm 16:11 (NLT)

What should I do with my life? Where do I live? Whom will I marry?…etc., etc. I can't stress to you enough to seek God about EVERY single thing you do! He has the perfect plan for you, my dear. Follow Him and you will be eternally HAPPY!

P.S. Don't forget to "ask" before you "do"!

PRAYER NOTES
for a
NEW BEGINNING

Today, God's Word spoke this to me_____

_____

_____

_____

_____

I will let go of_____

_____

_____

_____

_____

I will begin by_____

_____

_____

_____

[18] "Forget the former things; do not dwell on the past."

Isaiah 43:18 (NIV)

We moved a six-person family to two different states in just a five-month period. At the time, half of our family were teenagers, so you can just imagine the agony and the struggles within our family unit.

One morning, as I cried aloud to God, complaining about the moves, not being settled, our family unit falling apart, He pointed me to Exodus 14:14-15. God said, "My daughter, I Am taking care of you and your family. Now. . . GO FORWARD!" I received a peace that day and I have not looked back. Try it yourself! Nothing can be changed behind you, but everything CAN up ahead!

PRAYER NOTES
for a
NEW BEGINNING

Today, God's Word spoke this to me_____

_____

_____

_____

_____

I will let go of_____

_____

_____

_____

_____

I will begin by_____

_____

_____

_____

_____

¹⁹The Lord God is my Strength,
my personal bravery, and my invincible
army; He makes my feet like hinds' feet
and will make me to walk [not to stand
still in terror, but to walk] and make
[spiritual] progress upon my high places
[of trouble, suffering, or responsibility]!

Habakkuk 3:19 (AMP)

A Story of Determination:

*A donkey fell into a deep well. He struggled to escape, but to no avail.
The farmer, his master, heard the animal's cry and came running.
After watching the helpless donkey, he concluded that there was only
one thing to do. He grabbed his shovel and proceeded to toss dirt on top
of the donkey in an effort to bury him and put him out of his misery.
As each shovel of dirt hit the donkey's back, he shook it off and stepped
on top of the moving dirt. The donkey continued this until, at last, he
shook off the last shovel of dirt and stepped right out of that well!*

*Shake off that worry and torment, my friend, and use the strength of
God to step all over your places of suffering!*

PRAYER NOTES
for a
NEW BEGINNING

Today, God's Word spoke this to me_____

_____

_____

_____

_____

_____

I will let go of_____

_____

_____

_____

_____

_____

I will begin by_____

_____

_____

_____

_____

⁴Delight yourself also
in the LORD,
and He shall give you
the desires of your heart.

Psalm 37:4 (NKJV)

. . . *enough said!*

Titles by
June H. Olin
Rx for Happiness
Rx for Healing
Rx for Raising Teens

Watch for these upcoming titles:
Rx for Letting Go
Rx for Overcoming Fear
Rx for Financial Prosperity
Rx for Weight Control

For more information on ordering these books, write to:

Rx Books
PMB120
2020 Fieldstone Pkwy, Suite 900
Franklin, Tennessee 37069

Or e-mail Info@Rxbooks.com
www.Rxbooks.com